Texas Jack's Famous "How to Make Infused Vodka" Recipe Book: Over 70 Simple to Make Recipes

DENNIS WALLER

Disclaimer- This here book is for entertainment purposes only. Now, if you get a hankering to go out and turn into a Moonshiner based on what you learn in this book, well, I guess that's your business. But if a Revenuer like Eliot Ness comes a calling with a big old ax and a warrant, you're on your own and don't be going and implicating me any as the head honcho or ringleader. Causing if you do, well, I'll just have to remind you that I didn't tell you to do anything, other than enjoy this here book. But, if you do make up a batch of infused vodka that is downright good, I would be much obliged to have a taste or two. Now that we have all the legal stuff out of the way, let's get busy with making some infused vodka that Texas Jack would be proud of.

DEDICATION

To you, the reader. Thank you for purchasing this book and for your continued support, this one is for you because without you, there is no me then I would have to go get a real job.

CONTENTS

ACKNOWLEDGMENTS

"I love Texas and I love Vodka. When you put the two together, you get something oh so wonderful. Texas-Made Vodka"- Tito Beveridge

Thanks Tito for inspiring me

CHAPTER ONE
THE HISTORY OF VODKA

What is Vodka?

Before we begin discussing the history of vodka, let's take a look at what the US Federal Government has to say about it. The first thing you'll notice is the fact that vodka can be made from any ingredient that you can ferment, even something like molasses.

The U.S. Government definition of vodka reads as follows: Sec. 5.22 The standards of identity. Standards of identity for the several classes and types of distilled spirits set forth in this section shall be as follows (see also Sec. 5.35, class and type):

(a) Class 1: neutral spirits or alcohol. "Neutral spirits" or "alcohol" are distilled spirits produced from any material at or above 190 degrees, and, if bottled, bottled at not less than 80 proof.

(1) "Vodka" is neutral spirits so distilled, or so treated after distillation with charcoal or other materials, as to be without distinctive character, aroma, taste, or color.

After all that government talk just to say this about Vodka:

1- Made from any ingredient

2- Distilled at / above 190 degrees

3- Bottled at not less than 80 proof

As you can see from this vaguely basic definition, vodka can be and is, made up of all sorts of stuff and made in a variety of ways. Some distillers use some crazy stuff in the filtration of their vodka, from diamonds, river sand to charcoal.

With all of this said, you can see that not all vodkas are alike. It would pay to learn a little about how vodka is distilled and what filtration process distillers use. There is a stark difference in quality in the arena of vodka, from the low end brands to the top shelf brands.

Now, where were we? Oh yes, on the history of vodka.

A Brief History

It is said that vodka originated in the northern regions of Europe. The Polish have laid claim to being the first to discover this clear lightening. Well friends, I bet you the Russians have a thing or two to say about that. And, lest we forget about the Swedes. Yep, they lay claim to being the first too.

I guess the question here is, does it really matter? Not really, but what does matter, is ensuring getting the best you can get. However, that is another chapter. Back to these Big Three in the battle to being the first in "Vodka Crown." Interestingly, the word vodka comes from the word, *voda*, which means water in Russian. 1 point for the Russians.

The method used way back when was a process called "cold distilling." You see, the key to distillation is the separating the alcohol from the water content of the fermented liquid.

Because water freezes at a higher temperature than alcohol, folks were able to separate the alcohol by freezing their fermented liquid during the winter months. As a result of this process they were left with a higher strength of vodka than they could produce by fermentation alone. It is said that this method was accidently discovered in the eighth century in Poland when wine was left over during the winter to freeze thus giving a much stronger and higher alcohol content to the wine.

I know this process works and have used it myself in making hard apple cider and I discuss it in the book, "Texas Jack's Famous Apple Cider Recipes." It is simple, just place the liquid in the freezer and once a slush forms over the top, remove it and repeat till there isn't any more slush forming. At that point, you would have an alcohol content in the neighborhood of 35% to 40% and that folks isn't a soft beverage. This was the earliest method of producing stronger spirits back then.

You might be asking just what these folks were using to make vodka. Well, they used whatever local resources they had such as wheat, barley, ryes, potatoes and rice. Over the years as distilling and filtration techniques improved, local folks settled more on using wheat and potatoes however it is agreed that rye makes the best vodka except in Texas where corn is King in making vodka.

I would imagine in the middle of a hot summer during the 15th century when cold distilling was out definitely of the question, someone hit on the idea of distilling their mash with heat, sounds simple eh? Some say this new process was derive from gorzalka, or burnt wine. Well, we don't know who or when but some ingenuous soul figured it out and vodka as we know today was born. Through the process that was used on burnt wine, a new technology of using a pot-still emerged and it spread all over Europe like a wildfire. Polish historians claim that vodka made with this process was first produced in 1405 and reached Russia from Poland. 1 point for Poland.

Sweden really didn't play a big role like Russia and Poland during this time. The reason being is the Swedes were in the middle of a strong temperance movement. Well, with those folks running around condemning the virtues of the "drink" they were resigned to using vodka strictly for medicinal purposes. How much you want to bet there were a lot of sick folks in need of medicinal care.

However, our Puritans weren't to be outdone as there were multiple attempts to ban the production of vodka for health reasons, paradoxically speaking that is. Considering the condition of the Swedish culture, the powers that be decided that the revenue from taxing this elixir was far more significant and profitable than the culture's health. No points for Sweden.

In a maddening rush to improve the art of vodka making, somewhere along the 18th century, it was discovered that charcoal was an excellent method for filtrating vodka in order to get rid of the unnecessary and unpleasant by-products. It certainly worked better than the other mediums like river sand and felt that were the norm during this period. By this time, the spirits coming out of the pot-stills were approaching almost pure alcohol and soon discovered that it had to be diluted before it was filtered. Due to this new advancement in filtration, the practice of triple distillation came in to play. This process is still used today. It is said that the Russians were on the forefront of this amazing discovery. The Russians now have 2 points. You know what, because of the triple distillation, let's make that 3 points.

Fast forward to the 20th century, in the United States, Americans knew very little about vodka prior to World War II. Vodka was only known throughout Russian novels and movies about Czarist Russia where the likes of Peter the Great would serve massive quantities of vodka at his legendary banquets along with a bear or two running around on a unicycle.

All of this changed though after the war when servicemen brought back bottles of vodka from Europe. American capitalism not to be outdone started to import vodka from Europe. It wasn't too long before distilleries started making vodka here. And this is where I wrap this up and get to the point.

Tito's Handmade Vodka made by the Mockingbird Distilling Company in Austin Texas is generally known as the best U.S. vodka company in existence. Believe it or not but the creator of Tito's is none other than Tito Beveridge, no joke. Yes, that's his real name. Tito Beveridge, the geologist, yeah, a rock hound, is the founder and owner of Tito's Handmade Vodka, winner of multiple international awards for the best vodka in the world.

Even though it is based on Austin, Texas, the vodka can be found in every state in the U.S. The vodka is crafted in small batches and distilled six times. It was the first legal distillery in the state of Texas and remains the oldest. Its vodka is made exclusively from corn and is completely gluten free.

With that said, Texas wins with a runaway victory scoring 100 points, thus making Texas the champion in our little vodka contest. Yes, I know Texas wasn't the first to make vodka, but it is by far the best and isn't that what it's all about? Well sir, here in Texas, it does. Tito's Vodka and Texas, it just doesn't get any better than that.

CHAPTER TWO
INFUSED VODKAS

Infused vodkas have become very popular over the last few years. In fact, some would call it a rage within the industry. One look down the vodka aisle at any local liquor store will confirm that. From vanilla, root beer, marshmallow, to bacon, whatever you can think of, it's available at a store somewhere. Now days when you walk into a liquor store, there are entire rows dedicated to all the flavored vodkas produced by the leading makers of quality vodka. Some of these infused vodkas sell for a pretty penny too.

Well, good old Texas Jack has some great news for you. There is no need to buy these infused vodkas at the store. No sir. Infused vodkas are incredibly simple to make, even if you have no cooking skills. Doesn't matter if you don't know the difference between an egg flipper and a whisk, you'll be making your own infused vodka in no time. They are simple and relatively affordable to make. The only limit to creating your very own exotic flavors is your imagination.

Another plus to making your own infused vodka is you can make any amount you want. From a half pint to a gallon, whatever your heart desires, you can make it. Plus you can keep it organic and have control of what is in your infused vodka. No need to add any sugar mixtures, syrups, or any other stuff that isn't good for you.

Besides making better tasting flavored vodkas for your own use, infused vodkas make excellent gifts. Yes sir re bob, homemade infused vodkas are the perfect gift to give. Why, shoot fire, just send a bottle to Texas Jack and watch him smile. This is one gift that will surely please just about anyone you know that is known to take a sip now and then.

Texas Jack has some easy peasy simple step-by-step instructions for you to follow. With this book, you'll be well on your way to some delightfully good liquid merriment. Now, let's get busy with some book learning so you can start today making your good old friend, Texas Jack, a refreshing birthday present. So, when is his birthday you ask? Well now, when it comes to giving him a bottle of homemade infused vodka, every day is his birthday.

CHAPTER THREE
MAKING INFUSED VODKA

Making infused vodka is nothing more than adding an infusion of fruit, spice, vegetables, even candy or a combination of them to make a flavored vodka. The best thing about making infused vodka it's not an exact science. There are no rules as to what you can infuse so choose whatever combination you like and give it a try. Trust me; this is a very forgiving hobby and a very tasteful one too.

There are a few simple tips to keep in mind. Stronger flavored ingredients like pineapple take less time to infuse the vodka while mild flavored ingredients like pecans and almonds take longer. Some ingredients, as you'll see in the recipes, will be ready in just 24 hours. The thing is to keep an eye on your infusion by giving it a taste every now and then to see how it is coming along. When you reach the desired flavor, simply strain the infusion out and you're set to go.

Here are some general guidelines to help you determine the amount of time needed to get the desired results. Give citrus up to 3 days, more if using zest. Allow 3 to 4 days for fresh herbs and vanilla beans. Don't go too long with those vanilla beans or you'll end up with vanilla extract. Figure on a week for fruits like apples, pears, peaches, berries or other fruits with a mild flavor. When using spices like cinnamon sticks, fresh ginger, chili peppers, or jalapeno peppers, give them about 2 weeks.

When making infused vodka, I like using mason jars with tight fitting lids. The wide mouth makes it easy getting the fruit in the jar and easy to see. However, you can use whatever you like, just make sure you have a tight fitting seal on it. I know this doesn't need to be said, but make sure everything is cleaned and washed thoroughly before use.

Another thing you'll need is a good strainer or a sieve. I like straining my infused vodka twice. The first time I'll strain it through a strainer then through a sieve with a coffee filter. This is especially helpful if I am using spices or a puree. When using a coffee filter, rinse it with water first. This will help with getting the vodka through the filter without any waste. A dry coffee filter will adsorb a lot of the vodka, no sense letting all that hard work go to waste. If I am reusing the bottle the vodka came in, I use a funnel to keep the vodka where it belongs, in the bottle, not all over the counter. You don't need much in the way of tools and chances are, you already have these items in your kitchen. Remember clean vodka is good vodka.

Now, what brand of vodka should you use? Well, a rule of thumb is buy vodka that comes in a glass bottle. While it isn't necessary to use top shelf vodkas, you still want to use decent quality vodka. Look for vodkas that have been distilled at least six times.

Stay away from lower end vodkas that are packaged in plastic for two reasons. One, if it is in plastic, chances are it isn't a very good vodka that hasn't been distilled very many times. The more times a vodka has been distilled, the better the quality. Second, it is in a plastic bottle. With all the chemicals used in making plastic, you sure don't want any of that in your vodka.

I know what you are thinking. What brand of vodka does Texas Jack use? Well, being in Texas, "Tito's Vodka" is the only choice for me. Made in Austin and is the first legal distillery in Texas, (yep that is important, being legal and all.) Besides being made in Texas, Tito's Handmade Vodka is made from yellow corn, instead of the more commonly used wheat or potatoes, resulting in a mildly sweet aftertaste, and is distilled six times. Yep, this is one fine vodka that tastes great and it's priced right. This is the same vodka I use when making extracts such as vanilla and pecan. It is hard to beat Tito's for the quality and price. If you have Tito's available in your neck of the woods, give it a try, you'll be glad you did.

A General Set of Instructions to Making Infused Vodka

There will be specific instructions as needed for the different recipes like with the bacon infused vodka but these general instructions will just about apply to all the recipes in this book.

On the infusion ingredients, we'll get into that with the recipes; however here is a general guide to use. With using fresh herbs, give them a gentle crush to help in releasing their flavor. With fruits, it isn't necessary to peel them but ensure they are thoroughly clean, cored, and sliced before using. On grating zest, keep from using the white part or the pith as it is too bitter for our needs. With berries, it's okay to use them whole however I like slicing my strawberries to help releasing the flavor of the berries. On nuts like almonds or pecans, crush them but not too small. On peppers, cut them in half and remove the seeds. On vanilla beans, cut them in half. Remember, the more surface exposed to the vodka, the more flavor you'll get.

Make sure your containers are thoroughly washed and dried. I like to give them a nice rinse with a solution of 1 tablespoon of bleach to 1 gallon of water to ensure that my mason jars and lids are thoroughly sanitized.

Wash all produce you intend to infuse to remove pesticides or coatings. Now, if I am using apples, I will wash them in the same solution that I use to sanitize the containers. 1 tablespoon of bleach to 1 gallon of water will serve the purpose. It is important to give them a good wash to get all those pesticides off the skin.

Insert infusion ingredients in your container. For milder ingredients, fill the container halfway full. For stronger ingredients, use your judgment. Small fruits like berries may be left whole or puree to cut down on the infusion time, while bigger fruits like citrus, pears, mangoes, etc. can be sliced thinly or chopped.

Fill the rest of the container with vodka,(at least covering the top of the infusion) and put the lid on, ensuring it is sealed. If you are planning on making a smaller batch, use a smaller jar and cut up your fruits to fit.

Let the containers rest in a dark, cool place for the desired time. I keep mine in the pantry where it is out of direct sunlight and cool. Check on them every few days and shake up the bottles. And, don't be afraid to give them a taste.

If you're giving infused vodkas as a gift to be immediately enjoyed, you can leave the infusion ingredients in the jar for decorative purposes. However, if there's any chance your friend or family member will wait a while to drink them, (I wouldn't wait, heck, I'll have the top off before you know it) it's best to strain the ingredients out and re-bottle the vodka. If the ingredients sit for too long, they can turn the vodka bitter and downright nasty. So, it's your call. With that said, it does make for a nice gift, a mason jar of homemade Spiced Apple Infused Vodka with apple slices and a few cinnamon sticks left in the jar.

Make sure to label your infused vodkas as to not get confused with all the different flavors you make. The jars or bottles can be kept for up to two months in the refrigerator. Some folks keep them in the freezer, it's up to you. All I know, nothing is going to last that long around here, hehe.

Well, that's about it, now it's time to dive into the recipes and pick out your favorite and get started. Now, let me know how it works for you and please share with me any crazy combinations you come up with. Let's have some fun!

Tip- Conversion Table for converting milliliters into ounces

750 ml equals approximately 25 ounces or little over 3 cups

375 ml equals approximately 12.5 ounces or a little over 1 1/2 cups

CHAPTER FOUR
FRUIT AND VEGETABLE INFUSED VODKA RECIPES

Pomegranate Infused Vodka

This recipe is for a 750ml of vodka. You can adjust to make less if desired. You can also split this into two jars if you don't have a jar big enough to accommodate the recipe

Ingredients

3 ripe pomegranates

1 750ml bottle of vodka

Directions

Cut the pomegranates in half and scoop out the seeds. Place the seeds in a clean jar and fill with vodka. Seal the jar and place in a cool place away from direct sunlight for 5 to 7 days. Give the jar a shake every day and taste to see how the infusion is coming along. Once the infused vodka has attained the desired flavor, strain the fruit from the vodka and re-bottle. Keep refrigerated.

Strawberry Pomegranate Infused Vodka

This recipe is for a 750ml of vodka. You can adjust to make less if desired. You can also split this into two jars if you don't have a jar big enough to accommodate the recipe

Ingredients

2 cups ripe strawberries, washed, stems removed, and cut in half

3 ripe pomegranates

1 750ml bottle of vodka

Directions

Cut the pomegranates in half and scoop out the seeds. Place the seeds and prepared strawberries in a clean jar and fill with vodka. Seal the jar and place in a cool place away from direct sunlight for 5 to 7 days. Give the jar a shake every day and taste to see how the infusion is coming along. Once the infused vodka has attained the desired flavor, strain the fruit from the vodka and re-bottle. Keep refrigerated.

Pineapple Infused Vodka

This recipe is for a 750ml of vodka. You can adjust to make less if desired. You can also split this into two jars if you don't have a jar big enough to accommodate the recipe

Ingredients

2 cups ripe pineapple, washed, peeled, and chopped into 1 inch cubes

1 750ml bottle of vodka

Directions

Place the chopped pineapple in a clean jar and fill with vodka. Seal the jar and place in a cool place away from direct sunlight for 3 to 5 days. Give the jar a shake every day and taste to see how the infusion is coming along. Once the infused vodka has attained the desired flavor, strain the fruit from the vodka and re-bottle. Keep refrigerated.

Pineapple Coconut Infused Vodka

This recipe is for a 750ml of vodka. You can adjust to make less if desired. You can also split this into two jars if you don't have a jar big enough to accommodate the recipe

Ingredients

2 cups ripe pineapple, washed, peeled, and chopped into 1 inch cubes

1 cup sweeten coconut flakes

1 tablespoon coconut oil

1 750ml bottle of vodka

Directions

Place the chopped pineapple, coconut flakes and coconut oil in a clean jar and fill with vodka. Seal the jar and place in a cool place away from direct sunlight for 5 to 7 days. Give the jar a shake every day and taste to see how the infusion is coming along. Once the infused vodka has attained the desired flavor, strain the fruit from the vodka and re-bottle. Keep refrigerated.

Cranberry Infused Vodka

This recipe is for a 750ml of vodka. You can adjust to make less if desired. You can also split this into two jars if you don't have a jar big enough to accommodate the recipe

Ingredients

2 cups fresh or frozen cranberries, coarsely chopped

1 750ml bottle of vodka

Directions

Place the chopped cranberries in a clean jar and fill with vodka. Seal the jar and place in a cool place away from direct sunlight for 5 to 7 days. Give the jar a shake every day and taste to see how the infusion is coming along. You may allow the infusion to go longer to attain a stronger flavor. Once the infused vodka has attained the desired flavor, strain the fruit from the vodka and re-bottle. Keep refrigerated.

Orange Infused Vodka

This recipe is for a 750ml of vodka. You can adjust to make less if desired. You can also split this into two jars if you don't have a jar big enough to accommodate the recipe

Ingredients

2 cups fresh oranges, peeled and sliced

1 750ml bottle of vodka

Directions

Place the sliced oranges in a clean jar and fill with vodka. Seal the jar and place in a cool place away from direct sunlight for 3 to 5 days. Give the jar a shake every day and taste to see how the infusion is coming along. Once the infused vodka has attained the desired flavor, strain the fruit from the vodka and re-bottle. Keep refrigerated.

Orange Ginger Infused Vodka

This recipe is for a 750ml of vodka. You can adjust to make less if desired. You can also split this into two jars if you don't have a jar big enough to accommodate the recipe

Ingredients

2 cups fresh oranges, peeled and sliced

4 tablespoons fresh ginger root, peeled and coarsely chopped

1 750ml bottle of vodka

Directions

Place the sliced oranges and coarsely chopped ginger in a clean jar and fill with vodka. Seal the jar and place in a cool place away from direct sunlight for 5 to 7 days. Give the jar a shake every day and taste to see how the infusion is coming along. Once the infused vodka has attained the desired flavor, strain the fruit from the vodka and re-bottle. Keep refrigerated.

Spiced Blood Orange Infused Vodka

This recipe is for a 750ml of vodka. You can adjust to make less if desired. You can also split this into two jars if you don't have a jar big enough to accommodate the recipe

Ingredients

2 cups fresh Blood Oranges, peeled and sliced

2 cinnamon sticks, split down the middle

1 750ml bottle of vodka

Directions

Place the sliced blood oranges and cinnamon sticks in a clean jar and fill with vodka. Seal the jar and place in a cool place away from direct sunlight for 5 to 7 days. Give the jar a shake every day and taste to see how the infusion is coming along. Once the infused vodka has attained the desired flavor, strain the fruit from the vodka and re-bottle. Keep refrigerated.

Apple Infused Vodka

This recipe is for a 750ml of vodka. You can adjust to make less if desired. You can also split this into two jars if you don't have a jar big enough to accommodate the recipe

For a more tart apple vodka, use Granny Smith apples. For a sweeter apple vodka, use Pink Lady or Red Delicious

Ingredients

2 cups fresh apples, cored and sliced

1 750ml bottle of vodka

Directions

Place the cored and sliced apples in a clean jar and fill with vodka. Seal the jar and place in a cool place away from direct sunlight for 5 to 7 days. Give the jar a shake every day and taste to see how the infusion is coming along. Once the infused vodka has attained the desired flavor, strain the fruit from the vodka and re-bottle. Keep refrigerated.

Apple Cinnamon Infused Vodka

This recipe is for a 750ml of vodka. You can adjust to make less if desired. You can also split this into two jars if you don't have a jar big enough to accommodate the recipe

Ingredients

2 cups fresh apples, cored and sliced

4 sticks cinnamon, split down the middle

1 750ml bottle of vodka

Directions

Place the cored and sliced apples with the cinnamon sticks in a clean jar and fill with vodka. Seal the jar and place in a cool place away from direct sunlight for 5 to 7 days. Give the jar a shake every day and taste to see how the infusion is coming along. Once the infused vodka has attained the desired flavor, strain the fruit from the vodka and re-bottle. Keep refrigerated.

Spiced Apple Infused Vodka

This recipe is for a 750ml of vodka. You can adjust to make less if desired. You can also split this into two jars if you don't have a jar big enough to accommodate the recipe

Ingredients

2 cups fresh apples, cored and sliced

2 sticks cinnamon split down the middle

10 whole cloves

4 Allspice berries, crushed

2 tablespoons fresh ginger root, peeled and coarsely chopped

1 750ml bottle of vodka

Directions

Place the cored and sliced apples, cinnamon sticks, whole cloves, allspice berries, and ginger in a clean jar and fill with vodka. Seal the jar and place in a cool place away from direct sunlight for 5 to 7 days. Give the jar a shake every day and taste to see how the infusion is coming along. Once the infused vodka has attained the desired flavor, strain the fruit from the vodka and re-bottle. Keep refrigerated.

Spiced Pear Infused Vodka

This recipe is for a 750ml of vodka. You can adjust to make less if desired. You can also split this into two jars if you don't have a jar big enough to accommodate the recipe

Ingredients

2 cups fresh pears, peeled, cored and sliced

2 sticks cinnamon split down the middle

10 whole cloves

4 Allspice berries, crushed

2 tablespoons fresh ginger root, peeled and coarsely chopped

1 750ml bottle of vodka

Directions

Place the peeled, cored and sliced pears, cinnamon sticks, whole cloves, allspice berries, and ginger in a clean jar and fill with vodka. Seal the jar and place in a cool place away from direct sunlight for 5 to 7 days. Give the jar a shake every day and taste to see how the infusion is coming along. Once the infused vodka has attained the desired flavor, strain the fruit from the vodka and re-bottle. Keep refrigerated.

Mango Infused Vodka

This recipe is for a 750ml of vodka. You can adjust to make less if desired. You can also split this into two jars if you don't have a jar big enough to accommodate the recipe

Ingredients

2 large ripe sweet mangoes, washed, peeled, and sliced

1 750ml bottle of vodka

Directions

Place the sliced mangoes in a clean jar and fill with vodka. Ensure that the mangoes are sweet, if not, then get some that are. Whatever the flavor of the mangoes are, so will be the vodka. Seal the jar and place in a cool place away from direct sunlight for 5 to 7 days. Give the jar a shake every day and taste to see how the infusion is coming along. Once the infused vodka has attained the desired flavor, strain the fruit from the vodka and re-bottle. Keep refrigerated.

Mango Pineapple Coconut Infused Vodka

This recipe is for a 750ml of vodka. You can adjust to make less if desired. You can also split this into two jars if you don't have a jar big enough to accommodate the recipe

Ingredients

2 large ripe sweet mangoes, washed, peeled, and sliced

1 cup fresh pineapple, peeled and chopped into 1 inch cubes

½ cup sweeten coconut flakes

1 tablespoon coconut oil

1 750ml bottle of vodka

Directions

Place the sliced mangoes, chopped pineapple, coconut flakes, and coconut oil in a clean jar and fill with vodka. Ensure that the mangoes are sweet, if not, then get some that are. Whatever the flavor of the mangoes are, so will be the vodka. Seal the jar and place in a cool place away from direct sunlight for 5 to 7 days. Give the jar a shake every day and taste to see how the infusion is coming along. Once the infused vodka has attained the desired flavor, strain the fruit from the vodka and re-bottle. Keep refrigerated.

Coconut Infused Vodka

This recipe is for a 750ml of vodka. You can adjust to make less if desired. You can also split this into two jars if you don't have a jar big enough to accommodate the recipe

Ingredients

2 cups sweeten coconut flakes

2 tablespoons coconut oil

1 750ml bottle of vodka

Directions

Place the coconut flakes and oil in a clean jar and fill with vodka. Seal the jar and place in a cool place away from direct sunlight for 5 to 7 days. Give the jar a shake every day and taste to see how the infusion is coming along. Once the infused vodka has attained the desired flavor, strain the fruit from the vodka and re-bottle. Keep refrigerated.

Strawberry Infused Vodka

This recipe is for a 750ml of vodka. You can adjust to make less if desired. You can also split this into two jars if you don't have a jar big enough to accommodate the recipe

Ingredients

2 cups ripe strawberries, washed, stems removed, and cut in half

1 750ml bottle of vodka

Directions

Place the prepared strawberries in a clean jar and fill with vodka. Seal the jar and place in a cool place away from direct sunlight for 5 to 7 days. Give the jar a shake every day and taste to see how the infusion is coming along. Once the infused vodka has attained the desired flavor, strain the fruit from the vodka and re-bottle. Keep refrigerated.

Blueberry Infused Vodka

This recipe is for a 750ml of vodka. You can adjust to make less if desired. You can also split this into two jars if you don't have a jar big enough to accommodate the recipe

Ingredients

1 cup ripe blueberries, washed and lightly smashed

1 750ml bottle of vodka

Directions

Place the lightly smashed blueberries in a clean jar and fill with vodka. Seal the jar and place in a cool place away from direct sunlight for 5 to 7 days. Give the jar a shake every day and taste to see how the infusion is coming along. Once the infused vodka has attained the desired flavor, strain the fruit from the vodka and re-bottle. Keep refrigerated.

Very Berry Infused Vodka

This recipe is for a 750ml of vodka. You can adjust to make less if desired. You can also split this into two jars if you don't have a jar big enough to accommodate the recipe

Ingredients

1 cup strawberries, washed, stems removed and cut in half

1 cup ripe blueberries, washed and lightly smashed

½ cup raspberries, washed and lightly smashed

½ blackberries, washed and lightly smashed

1 750ml bottle of vodka

Directions

Place all the berries in a clean jar and fill with vodka. Seal the jar and place in a cool place away from direct sunlight for 5 to 7 days. Give the jar a shake every day and taste to see how the infusion is coming along. Once the infused vodka has attained the desired flavor, strain the fruit from the vodka and re-bottle. Keep refrigerated.

Cherry Infused Vodka

This recipe is for a 750ml of vodka. You can adjust to make less if desired. You can also split this into two jars if you don't have a jar big enough to accommodate the recipe

Ingredients

4 cups cherries, washed, pitted, stems removed and cut in half

1 750ml bottle of vodka

Directions

Place the cherries in a clean jar and fill with vodka. Seal the jar and place in a cool place away from direct sunlight for 5 to 7 days. Give the jar a shake every day and taste to see how the infusion is coming along. Once the infused vodka has attained the desired flavor, strain the fruit from the vodka and re-bottle. Keep refrigerated.

Watermelon Infused Vodka

This recipe is for a 750ml of vodka. You can adjust to make less if desired. You can also split this into two jars if you don't have a jar big enough to accommodate the recipe

Ingredients

4 cups sweet watermelon, chopped into cubes

1 750ml bottle of vodka

Directions

Place the watermelon in a clean jar and fill with vodka. Seal the jar and place in a cool place away from direct sunlight for 2 to 3 days. Give the jar a shake every day and taste to see how the infusion is coming along. Once the infused vodka has attained the desired flavor, strain the fruit from the vodka and re-bottle. Keep refrigerated.

Cantaloupe Infused Vodka

This recipe is for a 750ml of vodka. You can adjust to make less if desired. You can also split this into two jars if you don't have a jar big enough to accommodate the recipe

Ingredients

3 cups sweet cantaloupe, chopped into cubes

1 750ml bottle of vodka

Directions

Place the cantaloupe in a clean jar and fill with vodka. Seal the jar and place in a cool place away from direct sunlight for 2 to 3 days. Give the jar a shake every day and taste to see how the infusion is coming along. Once the infused vodka has attained the desired flavor, strain the fruit from the vodka and re-bottle. Keep refrigerated.

Honeydew Melon Infused Vodka

This recipe is for a 750ml of vodka. You can adjust to make less if desired. You can also split this into two jars if you don't have a jar big enough to accommodate the recipe

Ingredients

4 cups sweet honeydew melon, chopped into cubes

1 750ml bottle of vodka

Directions

Place the honeydew melon in a clean jar and fill with vodka. Seal the jar and place in a cool place away from direct sunlight for 2 to 3 days. Give the jar a shake every day and taste to see how the infusion is coming along. Once the infused vodka has attained the desired flavor, strain the fruit from the vodka and re-bottle. Keep refrigerated.

Cucumber Honeydew Melon Infused Vodka

This recipe is for a 750ml of vodka. You can adjust to make less if desired. You can also split this into two jars if you don't have a jar big enough to accommodate the recipe

Ingredients

2 large cucumbers, peeled and sliced

2 cups sweet honeydew melon, chopped into cubes

1 750ml bottle of vodka

Directions

Place the honeydew melon and cucumber in a clean jar and fill with vodka. Seal the jar and place in a cool place away from direct sunlight for 3 to 4 days. Give the jar a shake every day and taste to see how the infusion is coming along. Once the infused vodka has attained the desired flavor, strain the fruit from the vodka and re-bottle. Keep refrigerated.

Cucumber Infused Vodka

This recipe is for a 750ml of vodka. You can adjust to make less if desired. You can also split this into two jars if you don't have a jar big enough to accommodate the recipe

Ingredients

2 large cucumbers, peeled and sliced

1 tablespoon dried dill

1 750ml bottle of vodka

Directions

Place the peeled and sliced cucumbers and dried dill in a clean jar and fill with vodka. Seal the jar and place in a cool place away from direct sunlight for 5 to 7 days. Give the jar a shake every day and taste to see how the infusion is coming along. Once the infused vodka has attained the desired flavor, strain the fruit from the vodka and re-bottle. Keep refrigerated.

Cucumber Basil Infused Vodka

This recipe is for a 750ml of vodka. You can adjust to make less if desired. You can also split this into two jars if you don't have a jar big enough to accommodate the recipe

Ingredients

2 large cucumbers, peeled and sliced

1 small bunch fresh basil, wash and tear the leaves to release the flavor

1 750ml bottle of vodka

Directions

Place the peeled and sliced cucumbers and prepared basil leaves in a clean jar and fill with vodka. Seal the jar and place in a cool place away from direct sunlight for 5 to 7 days. Give the jar a shake every day and taste to see how the infusion is coming along. Once the infused vodka has attained the desired flavor, strain the fruit from the vodka and re-bottle. Keep refrigerated.

Cucumber Watermelon Infused Vodka

This recipe is for a 750ml of vodka. You can adjust to make less if desired. You can also split this into two jars if you don't have a jar big enough to accommodate the recipe

Ingredients

2 large cucumbers, peeled and sliced

2 cups sweet watermelon, chopped into cubes

Zest from one lemon

¼ cup fresh mint

½ teaspoon sea salt

1 750ml bottle of vodka

Directions

Place the watermelon, cucumber, lemon zest, fresh mint, and salt in a clean jar and fill with vodka. Seal the jar and place in the refrigerator for 7 to 14 days. Give the jar a shake every day and taste to see how the infusion is coming along. Once the infused vodka has attained the desired flavor, strain the ingredients from the vodka and re-bottle. Keep refrigerated.

Grapefruit Infused Vodka

This recipe is for a 750ml of vodka. You can adjust to make less if desired. You can also split this into two jars if you don't have a jar big enough to accommodate the recipe

Ingredients

1 large grapefruit, washed, and sliced into ½ inch slices

1 750ml bottle of vodka

Directions

Place the sliced grapefruit in a clean jar and fill with vodka. Seal the jar and place in a cool place away from direct sunlight for 2 to 3 days. Give the jar a shake every day and taste to see how the infusion is coming along. Once the infused vodka has attained the desired flavor, strain the fruit from the vodka and re-bottle. Keep refrigerated.

Lemon Infused Vodka

This recipe is for a 750ml of vodka. You can adjust to make less if desired. You can also split this into two jars if you don't have a jar big enough to accommodate the recipe

Ingredients

4 lemons, washed, and sliced into ½ inch slices

1 750ml bottle of vodka

Directions

Place the sliced lemons in a clean jar and fill with vodka. Seal the jar and place in a cool place away from direct sunlight for 2 to 3 days. Give the jar a shake every day and taste to see how the infusion is coming along. Once the infused vodka has attained the desired flavor, strain the fruit from the vodka and re-bottle. Keep refrigerated.

Lemon Lime Infused Vodka

This recipe is for a 750ml of vodka. You can adjust to make less if desired. You can also split this into two jars if you don't have a jar big enough to accommodate the recipe

Ingredients

2 lemons, washed and sliced into ½ inch slices

3 limes, washed and sliced into ½ slices

1 750ml bottle of vodka

Directions

Place the sliced lemons and limes in a clean jar and fill with vodka. Seal the jar and place in a cool place away from direct sunlight for 2 to 3 days. Give the jar a shake every day and taste to see how the infusion is coming along. Once the infused vodka has attained the desired flavor, strain the fruit from the vodka and re-bottle. Keep refrigerated.

Zesty Citrus Infused Vodka

This recipe is for a 750ml of vodka. You can adjust to make less if desired. You can also split this into two jars if you don't have a jar big enough to accommodate the recipe

Ingredients

Zest from 4 oranges

Zest from 1 lemon

Zest from 1 lime

Zest from 1 grapefruit

2 sticks cinnamon

6 whole cloves

2 tablespoons fresh ginger, peeled and grated

1 750ml bottle of vodka

Directions

Preheat oven to 200 degrees. Place all the zest from the citrus on a cookie sheet and bake for approximately one hour or until completely dry. Remove from oven and cool to room temperature.

Place the zest, whole cloves, grated ginger, and cinnamon in a clean jar and fill with vodka. Seal the jar and place in a cool place away from direct sunlight for 7 to 10 days. Give the jar a shake every day and taste to see how the infusion is coming along. Once the infused vodka has attained the desired flavor, strain the zest and spices from the vodka and re-bottle. Keep refrigerated.

NOTES

CHAPTER FIVE
HERB AND SPICE BASED INFUSED VODKA

Caraway Seed Infused Vodka

This recipe is for a 375ml of vodka. You can adjust to make less if desired.

Ingredients

4 tablespoons caraway seeds, lightly crushed

1 375ml bottle of vodka

Directions

Place the lightly crushed caraway seeds in a clean jar and fill with vodka. Seal the jar and place in a cool place away from direct sunlight for 14 to 21 days. Give the jar a shake every day and taste to see how the infusion is coming along. Once the infused vodka has attained the desired flavor, strain the seeds from the vodka and re-bottle.

Anise Infused Vodka

For a rich licorice flavor, try this recipe using anise stars. For a stronger flavor, add another tablespoon of anise extract and 2 more anise stars

This recipe is for a 375ml of vodka. You can adjust to make less if desired.

Ingredients

4 Anise Stars

1 tablespoon anise extract

1 375ml bottle of vodka

Directions

Place the anise stars and extract in a clean jar and fill with vodka. Seal the jar and place in a cool place away from direct sunlight for 14 to 21 days. Give the jar a shake every day and taste to see how the infusion is coming along. Once the infused vodka has attained the desired flavor, strain the anise stars from the vodka and re-bottle.

Coriander Lemon Infused Vodka

This recipe is for a 375ml of vodka. You can adjust to make less if desired.

Ingredients

2 tablespoons coriander seeds, lightly crushed

Zest from 2 lemons

1 375ml bottle of vodka

Directions

Place the lightly crushed coriander seeds and lemon zest in a clean jar and fill with vodka. Seal the jar and place in a cool place away from direct sunlight for 14 to 21 days. Give the jar a shake every day and taste to see how the infusion is coming along. Once the infused vodka has attained the desired flavor, strain the ingredients from the vodka and re-bottle.

Cardamom Ginger Infused Vodka

This recipe is for a 375ml of vodka. You can adjust to make more or less if desired.

Ingredients

12 Cardamom pods, lightly crushed

¼ cup fresh ginger, peeled and chopped

1 375ml bottle of vodka

Directions

Place the lightly crushed cardamom pods and fresh ginger in a clean jar and fill with vodka. Seal the jar and place in a cool place away from direct sunlight for 14 to 21 days. Give the jar a shake every day and taste to see how the infusion is coming along. Once the infused vodka has attained the desired flavor, strain the ingredients from the vodka and re-bottle.

Cilantro Lime Infused Vodka

This recipe is for a 375ml of vodka. You can adjust to make less if desired.

Ingredients

1/3 cup fresh cilantro, lightly crushed

Zest from 1 lime

1 375ml bottle of vodka

Directions

Place the lightly crushed cilantro and lime zest in a clean jar and fill with vodka. Seal the jar and place in a cool place away from direct sunlight for 7 to 10 days. Give the jar a shake every day and taste to see how the infusion is coming along. It's okay to let this one go a little longer to achieve a stronger flavor. Once the infused vodka has attained the desired flavor, strain the ingredients from the vodka and re-bottle.

Clove Orange Infused Vodka

This recipe is for a 375ml of vodka. You can adjust to make less if desired.

Ingredients

12 whole cloves

Zest from 1 orange

1 375ml bottle of vodka

Directions

Place the whole cloves and orange zest in a clean jar and fill with vodka. Seal the jar and place in a cool place away from direct sunlight for 7 to 10 days. Give the jar a shake every day and taste to see how the infusion is coming along. Once the infused vodka has attained the desired flavor, strain the ingredients from the vodka and re-bottle.

Celery Bay Leaf Infused Vodka

This recipe is for a 375ml of vodka. You can adjust to make less if desired.

This infused vodka has hints of Amaretto that works well in several drink recipes

Ingredients

1/3 cup sliced celery tops (the leave portion of the celery)

6 dried Bay leafs

½ teaspoon peppercorns

1 375ml bottle of vodka

Directions

Place the celery, bay leafs and peppercorns in a clean jar and fill with vodka. Seal the jar and place in a cool place away from direct sunlight for 3 to 5 days. Give the jar a shake every day and taste to see how the infusion is coming along. Once the infused vodka has attained the desired flavor, strain the ingredients from the vodka and re-bottle.

Basil Infused Vodka

This recipe is for a 750ml of vodka. You can adjust to make less if desired.

This infused vodka has hints of Amaretto that works well in several drink recipes

Ingredients

1 large bunch of fresh basil leaves

2 dried Bay leafs

½ teaspoon fennel seeds

1 375ml bottle of vodka

Directions

Place the basil, bay leafs and fennel seeds in a clean jar and fill with vodka. Seal the jar and place in a cool place away from direct sunlight for 5 to 7 days. Give the jar a shake every day and taste to see how the infusion is coming along. Once the infused vodka has attained the desired flavor, strain the ingredients from the vodka and re-bottle.

Dill Infused Vodka

This recipe is for a 375ml of vodka. You can adjust to make less if desired.

Ingredients

1 small bunch of fresh dill, coarsely chopped

1 375ml bottle of vodka

Directions

Place the coarsely chopped dill in a clean jar and fill with vodka. Seal the jar and place in a cool place away from direct sunlight for 3 to 5 days. Give the jar a shake every day and taste to see how the infusion is coming along. Once the infused vodka has attained the desired flavor, strain the dill from the vodka and re-bottle.

Cilantro and Pomegranate Infused Vodka

This recipe is for a 375ml of vodka. You can adjust to make less if desired.

These two ingredients pair very well together and works rather well in a margarita

Ingredients

1 small bunch of fresh cilantro, coarsely chopped

½ of a ripe pomegranate,

1 375ml bottle of vodka

Directions

Cut the pomegranate in half and scoop out the seeds from one half. Place the pomegranate seeds and coarsely chopped cilantro in a clean jar and fill with vodka. Seal the jar and place in a cool place away from direct sunlight for 3 to 5 days. Give the jar a shake every day and taste to see how the infusion is coming along. Once the infused vodka has attained the desired flavor, strain the ingredients from the vodka and re-bottle.

Lemongrass and Lime Infused Vodka

This recipe is for a 750ml of vodka. You can adjust to make less if desired.

Ingredients

1 large bunch of fresh lemongrass

Zest from one lime

1 750ml bottle of vodka

Directions

Place the lemongrass and lime zest in a clean jar and fill with vodka. Seal the jar and place in a cool place away from direct sunlight for 5 to 7 days. Give the jar a shake every day and taste to see how the infusion is coming along. Once the infused vodka has attained the desired flavor, strain the ingredients from the vodka and re-bottle.

NOTES

CHAPTER SIX
CANDY BASED INFUSED VODKA

Peppermint Infused Vodka

This recipe is for a 750ml of vodka. You can adjust to make less if desired. You can also split this into two jars if you don't have a jar big enough to accommodate the recipe

Ingredients

1 cup peppermint hard candies

1 750ml bottle of vodka

Directions

Place the unwrapped peppermint candies in a clean jar and fill with vodka. Seal the jar and place in a cool place away from direct sunlight for 7 to 10 days. Give the jar a shake every day and taste to see how the infusion is coming along. Once the infused vodka has attained the desired flavor, strain the fruit from the vodka and re-bottle. Keep refrigerated.

Marshmallow Infused Vodka

This recipe is for a 750ml of vodka. You can adjust to make less if desired. You can also split this into two jars if you don't have a jar big enough to accommodate the recipe.

When I make my marshmallow infused vodka, I like using a 10.5 ounce package of mini marshmallows. You can use the large marshmallows if you like but I like using the minis to maximize the infusion of the flavor. This recipe doesn't take very long so make sure to stay on top of it. I would recommend tasting the vodka after 24 hours and if the flavor is there, go ahead and strain it. If not, go another 12 hours.

Ingredients

1 package mini marshmallows, between 10.5 and 12 ounces

1 750ml bottle of vodka

Directions

Place the mini marshmallows into two clean jars and fill with vodka. Seal the jar and place in a cool place away from direct sunlight for 24 hours. Give the vodka a taste after 24 hours to see if you have achieved the desired flavor. If not, allow another 12 hours. Once the infused vodka has attained the desired flavor, strain the marshmallows from the vodka and re-bottle. Keep refrigerated.

Jolly Rancher Infused Vodka

This recipe is for a 375ml of vodka. You can adjust to make less if desired.

This is a fun infused vodka to make using Jolly Rancher hard candies. What makes this so interesting are all the different flavors to choose from. Some of the favorite flavors are Cherry, Blue Raspberry, Strawberry, Watermelon, Sour Apple, Apple, Peach, and Orange Tangerine with the Watermelon and Sour Apple being my personal favorites. Imagine having your own Sour Apple Infused Vodka to use in your martinis. Oh yeah, I betcha this recipe is going to become a favorite of yours once you give it a try.

Ingredients

24 pieces of Jolly Rancher Hard Candy, all the same flavor

1 375ml bottle of vodka

Directions

Place the Jolly Rancher hard candy in a clean jar and fill with vodka. Seal the jar and shake really well until contents are thoroughly mixed. Place in a cool place away from direct sunlight for 24 to 48 hours or until the candies are fully dissolved. Give the jar a shake every now and then. Once the candies have dissolved, strain the vodka through a coffee filter to remove the ingredients and re-bottle.

Double Bubble Gum Infused Vodka

This recipe is for a 375ml of vodka. You can adjust to make less if desired.

Another interesting recipe as there are so many different flavors of bubble gum to choose from. If you are looking for that classic taste of bubble gum, for me, there is only one and that is the Original Double Bubble Gum. However, experiment with them all to find the one that will become your favorite.

Ingredients

1cup double bubble gum or similar type of bubble gum

1 375ml bottle of vodka

Directions

Place the bubble gum in a clean jar and fill with vodka. Seal the jar and shake really well until contents are thoroughly mixed. Place in a cool place away from direct sunlight for 24 to 48 hours or until you have the desired flavor. It's okay to let this go a few extra days. Give the jar a shake every now and then. Once you have achieved the desired taste, strain the vodka through a coffee filter to remove the ingredients and re-bottle.

Red Hot Cinnamon Infused Vodka

This recipe is for a 375ml of vodka. You can adjust to make less if desired.

Another fun recipe that is sure to become a favorite among your friends and so easy to make and have ready on a moment's notice.

Ingredients

1cup cinnamon red hot candies, crushed by hand or in a food processor

1 375ml bottle of vodka

Directions

Place the cinnamon red hot candies in a clean jar and fill with vodka. Seal the jar and shake really well until contents are thoroughly mixed. Place in a cool place away from direct sunlight for 24 to 48 hours or until you have the desired flavor. It's okay to let this go a few extra days. Give the jar a shake every now and then. Once you have achieved the desired taste, strain the vodka through a coffee filter to remove the ingredients and re-bottle.

Root Beer Infused Vodka

This recipe is for a 375ml of vodka. You can adjust to make less if desired.

A fun infused vodka to make using Root Beer flavored hard candies. A few of my personal favorites are Dad's, IBC, and Claeys which you can find at any Cracker Barrel Restaurant. Imagine having your own Root Beer Infused Vodka to use in your martinis. Oh yeah, I like this one with the Marshmallow Infused Vodka with a shot of Big Red soda.

Ingredients

24 pieces of Root Beer flavored Hard Candy

1 375ml bottle of vodka

Directions

Place the Root Beer flavored hard candy in a clean jar and fill with vodka. Seal the jar and shake really well until contents are thoroughly mixed. Place in a cool place away from direct sunlight for 24 to 48 hours or until the candies are fully dissolved. You can give this one more time if you like to get a stronger flavor. Give the jar a shake every now and then. Once the candies have dissolved, strain the vodka through a coffee filter to remove the ingredients and re-bottle.

Haribo Coca Infused Vodka

This recipe is for a 375ml of vodka. You can adjust to make less if desired.

A fun infused vodka to make using Gummy Bears. This is one with a lot of options as you can use any flavor of gummy bears you like. For this recipe, we are using Haribo Coca Gummy Bears to make a Coca flavored infuses vodka.

Ingredients

1 cup of Haribo Coca Gummy Bears

1 375ml bottle of vodka

Directions

Place 1 cup of Gummy Bears in a clean jar and fill with vodka. Seal the jar and shake really well until contents are thoroughly mixed. Place in a cool place away from direct sunlight for 24 to 48 hours. Don't let this go too long as the gummy bears will turn into a mess. Give the infusion a taste every few hours and once you have the desired flavor, strain the vodka through a coffee filter to remove the ingredients and re-bottle.

Werther's Caramel Apple Infused Vodka

This recipe is for a 375ml of vodka. You can adjust to make less if desired.

Who doesn't love Werther's hard candy? Their caramel candy is one of the best on the market. Werther's has in addition to their traditional caramel, have caramel apple, coffee caramel and caramel cinnamon among others. Give all the flavors made by Werther's a try, you might be surprised.

Ingredients

24 pieces of Werther's hard candy, crushed

1 375ml bottle of vodka

Directions

Place the candy in a zip-lock bag and crush into small pieces. This will help in expediting the infusion process. Place the crushed candy in a clean jar and fill with vodka. Seal the jar and shake really well until contents are thoroughly mixed. Place in a cool place away from direct sunlight for 24 to 48 hours. It's okay to let this go for a few extra days to get the desired flavor. Once the candies have nearly dissolved, strain the vodka through a coffee filter to remove the ingredients and re-bottle.

Brach's Butterscotch Infused Vodka

This recipe is for a 375ml of vodka. You can adjust to make less if desired.

Ingredients

24 pieces of Brach's Butterscotch hard candy, crushed

1 375ml bottle of vodka

Directions

Take the candies and place them in a zip-lock bag and crush into small pieces. This will help in expediting the infusion process. Place the crush candy in a clean jar and fill with vodka. Seal the jar and shake really well until contents are thoroughly mixed. Place in a cool place away from direct sunlight for 24 to 48 hours. It's okay to let this go for a few extra days to get the desired flavor. Give the jar a shake every now and then. Once the candies have nearly dissolved, strain the vodka through a coffee filter to remove the ingredients and re-bottle.

Starburst Fruit Chews Infused Vodka

This recipe is for a 375ml of vodka. You can adjust to make less if desired.

Starburst is another great candy that offers a wide selection of flavors. Their original flavors are strawberry, orange, lemon and cherry. Then there are mango melon, pina colada, strawberry banana, watermelon, and more. The combinations are endless with using Starburst Fruit Chews in making an original flavored infused vodka.

Ingredients

12 pieces of Starburst Fruit Chews

1 375ml bottle of vodka

Directions

Place the candy in a clean jar and fill with vodka. Seal the jar and shake really well until contents are thoroughly mixed. Place in the refrigerator for 24 to 48 hours. Once the candies have dissolved, strain the vodka through a coffee filter to remove the ingredients and re-bottle.

CHAPTER SEVEN
UNIQUE BASED INFUSED VODKA

Praline Infused Vodka

This recipe is for a 750ml of vodka. You can adjust to make less if desired.

Ingredients

2 cups pecans, chopped

1 tablespoon pecan extract (optional)

1 vanilla bean, split down the middle

¼ cup brown sugar

2 tablespoons powdered white sugar

1 750ml bottle of vodka

Directions

Place the pecans, vanilla bean, extract, and sugars in a clean jar and fill with vodka. Seal the jar and shake really well until contents are thoroughly mixed. Place in a cool place away from direct sunlight for 21 to 28 days. Give the jar a shake every other day and taste to see how the infusion is coming along. Once the infused vodka has attained the desired flavor, strain the vodka through a coffee filter to remove the ingredients and re-bottle.

Bacon Infused Vodka

This recipe is for a 750ml of vodka. You can adjust to make less if desired. You can also split this into two jars if you don't have a jar big enough to accommodate the recipe.

One point to keep in mind when using bacon is the type of bacon will affect the infusion. If you want a smokier flavor, then use a hickory smoked bacon. For a more subtle sweet flavor, try using an apple-wood smoked bacon or a maple bacon. For a spicy flavor, try using peppered bacon or Gypsy bacon. Feel free to experiment with different types of bacon to attain the flavor that you like.

Ingredients

8 strips of bacon

1 750ml bottle of vodka

Directions

Fry the bacon strips in a skillet until done. Remove from the skillet and place on a paper towel to absorb the grease. Once cooled and dry, place the bacon into a clean jar and fill with vodka. Seal the jar and place in the refrigerator for 7 days. Give the vodka a taste after the allotted time to see if you have achieved the desired flavor. If not, allow another 3 days. Once the infused vodka has attained the desired flavor, strain the bacon from the vodka and re-bottle. Keep refrigerated.

Spicy Bacon Infused Vodka

This recipe is for a 750ml of vodka. You can adjust to make less if desired. You can also split this into two jars if you don't have a jar big enough to accommodate the recipe.

One point to keep in mind when using bacon is the type of bacon will affect the infusion. If you want a smokier flavor, then use a hickory smoked bacon. For a more subtle sweet flavor, try using an apple-wood smoked bacon or a maple bacon. For a spicy flavor, try using peppered bacon or Gypsy bacon. Feel free to experiment with different types of bacon to attain the flavor that you like.

Ingredients

8 strips of bacon

1 jalapeno pepper cut in half and seeds removed

2 chili de arbol peppers, these are dried red chilies and hot, lightly crushed

1 750ml bottle of vodka

Directions

Fry the bacon strips in a skillet until done. Remove from the skillet and place on a paper towel to absorb the grease. Once cooled and dry, place the bacon into a clean jar along with the jalapeno pepper and the crushed chili de arbol peppers and fill with vodka. Seal the jar and place in the refrigerator for 7 days.

Give the vodka a taste after the allotted time to see if you have achieved the desired flavor. If not, allow another 3 days. Once the infused vodka has attained the desired flavor, strain the bacon and peppers from the vodka and re-bottle. Keep refrigerated.

Spicy Bacon Tomato Infused Vodka

This recipe is for a 750ml of vodka. You can adjust to make less if desired. You can also split this into two jars if you don't have a jar big enough to accommodate the recipe.

One point to keep in mind when using bacon is the type of bacon will affect the infusion. If you want a smokier flavor, then use a hickory smoked bacon. For a more subtle sweet flavor, try using an apple-wood smoked bacon or a maple bacon. For a spicy flavor, try using peppered bacon or Gypsy bacon. Feel free to experiment with different types of bacon to attain the flavor that you like.

Ingredients

8 strips of bacon

1 jalapeno pepper cut in half and seeds removed

2 chili de arbol peppers, these are dried red chilies and hot, lightly crushed

2 cups cherry tomatoes washed and cut in half. You may use any type of tomato though

2 tablespoons peppercorns

1 tablespoon dried basil

1/4 teaspoon fresh garlic, crushed

1 750ml bottle of vodka

Directions

Fry the bacon strips in a skillet until done. Remove from the skillet and place on a paper towel to absorb the grease. Once cooled and dry, place the bacon into a clean jar along with the jalapeno pepper, crushed chili de arbol peppers, peppercorns, basil, garlic, and the tomatoes and fill with vodka. Seal the jar and place in the refrigerator for 7 days. Give the vodka a taste after the allotted time to see if you have achieved the desired flavor. If not, allow another 3 days. Once the infused vodka has attained the desired flavor, strain the ingredients from the vodka and re-bottle. Keep refrigerated.

Almond Apricot Infused Vodka

This recipe is for a 375ml of vodka. You can adjust to make less if desired.

This infused vodka has hints of Amaretto that works well in several drink recipes

Ingredients

½ cup sliced almonds

4 pieces dried apricot

1 teaspoon almond extract

1 375ml bottle of vodka

Directions

Place the sliced almonds, dried apricots, and extract in a clean jar and fill with vodka. Seal the jar and place in a cool place away from direct sunlight for 7 to 10 days. Give the jar a shake every day and taste to see how the infusion is coming along. Once the infused vodka has attained the desired flavor, strain the ingredients from the vodka and re-bottle.

Chili Spiced Mango Infused Vodka

This recipe is for a 750ml of vodka. You can adjust to make less if desired. You can also split this into two jars if you don't have a jar big enough to accommodate the recipe

Ingredients

2 large mangoes, peeled and sliced

Zest from one orange

Zest from one lime

2 chili de arbol peppers, crushed

½ teaspoon paprika

½ teaspoon cayenne pepper

1 750ml bottle of vodka

Directions

Place the mangoes, zest, crushed peppers, and spices in a clean jar and fill with vodka. Seal the jar and place in the refrigerator for 7 to 14 days. Give the jar a shake every day and taste to see how the infusion is coming along. Once the infused vodka has attained the desired flavor, strain the ingredients from the vodka and re-bottle. Keep refrigerated.

Spiced Pumpkin Infused Vodka

This recipe is for a 750ml of vodka. You can adjust to make less if desired. You can also split this into two jars if you don't have a jar big enough to accommodate the recipe

Ingredients

2 cups pumpkin, peeled and cubed

Zest from half of an orange

1 whole nutmeg, lightly crushed

6 whole cloves

2 cinnamon sticks, split in half

2 tablespoons fresh grated ginger

6 whole allspice balls, lightly crushed

1/2 vanilla bean, split down the middle

1 750ml bottle of vodka

Directions

Place the pumpkin, zest, and spices in a clean jar and fill with vodka. Seal the jar and place in a cool place out of direct sunlight for 14 to 21 days. Give the jar a shake every day and taste to see how the infusion is coming along. Once the infused vodka has attained the desired flavor, strain the ingredients from the vodka and re-bottle. Keep refrigerated.

Johnny Cash's "Sunday Morning Coming Down" Infused Vodka

This recipe is for a 750ml of vodka. You can adjust to make less if desired. You can also split this into two jars if you don't have a jar big enough to accommodate the recipe.

In honor of the man himself, here is my homage to Johnny Cash with a recipe that is most excellent on a Sunday morning after a more than busy Saturday night.

Ingredients

3 ounces canned kippered herring, drained

8 strips of bacon

1 jalapeno pepper cut in half and seeds removed

2 chili de arbol peppers, these are dried red chilies and hot, lightly crushed

2 cups cherry tomatoes washed and cut in half. You may use any type of tomato though

2 celery stalks, chopped

2 tablespoons peppercorns

1 tablespoon dried basil

1/4 teaspoon fresh garlic, crushed

1 750ml bottle of vodka

Directions

Fry the bacon strips in a skillet until done. Remove from the skillet and place on a paper towel to absorb the grease. Drain the kippered herring to remove as much oil as possible. Once cooled and dry, place the bacon and kippered herring into a clean jar along with the jalapeno pepper, crushed chili de arbol peppers, peppercorns, basil, celery, garlic, and the tomatoes and fill with vodka. Seal the jar and place in the refrigerator for 7 days. Give the vodka a taste after the allotted time to see if you have achieved the desired flavor. If not, allow another 3 days. Once the infused vodka has attained the desired flavor, strain the ingredients from the vodka and re-bottle. Keep refrigerated.

Sunday Morning Coming Down Cocktail

2 ounces of "Sunday Morning Coming Down" Infused Vodka

8 ounces of Original V8 juice

A dash of hot sauce and

A dash of Worcestershire sauce

One stalk of celery

Pinch of salt and pepper (optional)

Directions

Thoroughly stir ingredients by pouring between two mixing glasses. Pour into tall glass with ice and garnish with a celery stalk. This will bring a whole new meaning to a bloody mary.

CHAPTER EIGHT
CHOCOLATE, COFFEE AND TEA INFUSED VODKA

"Republic of Tea" Infused Vodka Series of Recipes

Republic of Tea is a brand of tea that offers a wide variety of loose leaf, bagged, and flavored teas. Their quality is excellent as well as their selection. I encourage you to check out their website to get some ideas on making some really incredible infused vodka. There are other brands of tea out there too and feel free to experiment. However for the sake of the argument, I have provided a list of their teas to give you an insight into the possibilities. Here is the link to their website: www.republicoftea.com

Ginger Peach – Strawberry Basil Green Tea - Hibiscus Watermelon – Watermelon Mint

Pineapple Orange Guava – Raspberry Rose Hibiscus – Cardamom Cinnamon

Organic Turmeric Ginger Green Tea – Blackberry Sage – Orange Ginger Mint

Wild Blueberry – Cranberry Blood Orange – Peppermint Cuppa Chocolate

Pomegranate Green Tea – Honey Ginseng – Jasmine Jazz Green Tea

This recipe is for a 750ml of vodka. You can adjust to make less if desired. You can also split this into two jars if you don't have a jar big enough to accommodate the recipe

Ingredients

4 tea bags of your flavor

1 750ml bottle of vodka

Directions

Place the tea bags in a clean jar and fill with vodka. Seal the jar and give it a good shake. Place on the counter for 3 to 5 hours. Once the infused vodka has attained the desired flavor, remove the tea bags and strain the vodka and re-bottle. Keep refrigerated.

Black Tea Infused Vodka

This recipe is for a 750ml of vodka. You can adjust to make less if desired. You can also split this into two jars if you don't have a jar big enough to accommodate the recipe

Ingredients

1 heaping tablespoon loose leaf black tea

1 750ml bottle of vodka

Directions

Place the loose leaf black tea in a clean jar and fill with vodka. Seal the jar and give it a good shake. Place on the counter for 3 to 5 hours. Once the infused vodka has attained the desired flavor, strain the black tea from the vodka and re-bottle. Keep refrigerated.

Chocolate Infused Vodka

This recipe is for a 750ml of vodka. You can adjust to make less if desired. The key to achieving a high quality chocolate infused vodka is in the quality of cocoa powder you use. Strive to get the best you can in cocoa powder. Ghirardelli makes a good quality cocoa powder and Scharffen Berger is a good one too. If you are having a hard time finding these, check out Amazon for a wide selection of quality cocoa powders.

Ingredients

1 cup cocoa powder

1 750ml bottle of vodka

Directions

Place the cup of cocoa powder in a clean jar and fill with vodka. Seal the jar and shake really well until contents are thoroughly mixed. Place in a cool place away from direct sunlight for 21 to 28 days. Give the jar a shake every other day and taste to see how the infusion is coming along. Once the infused vodka has attained the desired flavor, strain the vodka through a coffee filter and re-bottle.

Chocolate Mint Infused Vodka

This recipe is for a 750ml of vodka. You can adjust to make less if desired. The key to achieving a high quality chocolate infused vodka is in the quality of cocoa powder you use. Strive to get the best you can in cocoa powder. Ghirardelli makes a good quality cocoa powder and Scharffen Berger is a good one too. If you are having a hard time finding these, check out Amazon for a wide selection of quality cocoa powders.

Ingredients

1 cup cocoa powder

¼ cup fresh mint, washed and chopped

1 750ml bottle of vodka

Directions

Place the cup of cocoa powder and fresh mint in a clean jar and fill with vodka. Seal the jar and shake really well until contents are thoroughly mixed. Place in a cool place away from direct sunlight for 21 to 28 days. Give the jar a shake every other day and taste to see how the infusion is coming along. Once the infused vodka has attained the desired flavor, strain the vodka through a coffee filter to remove the mint and any residue from the cocoa powder and re-bottle.

Coffee Infused Vodka

This recipe is for a 750ml of vodka. You can adjust to make less if desired. The key to achieving a high quality coffee infused vodka is in the quality of coffee beans you use. You can pick up your favorite beans from your grocery store or even at a Starbucks. Dark roasted beans have a stronger flavor which in turn gives a stronger infusion. However, use whatever beans you like. One key to infusing coffee beans is to crack open the beans, not necessarily crush them. If you like your coffee vodka to have a sweet taste, add sugar to the recipe to taste after the infusion.

Ingredients

1/2 cup dark roasted coffee beans, lightly cracked

1/4 cup sugar, optional

1 750ml bottle of vodka

Directions

Place the cracked coffee beans in a clean jar and fill with vodka. Seal the jar and shake really well until contents are thoroughly mixed. Place in a cool place away from direct sunlight for 12 to 48 hours. Give the infusion a taste to see how the infusion is coming along. Once the infused vodka has attained the desired flavor, strain the vodka through a coffee filter to remove the ingredients and re-bottle.

Note: For an added flavor, you can add 2 tablespoons of vanilla extract to the infusion once you have strain it. You can also substitute the white sugar with brown sugar. Adding vanilla and brown sugar tones down the coffee and gives it a Kahlua-esque flavor. You can always pour out a small quantity and experiment.

Mexican Chili Mocha Infused Vodka

This recipe is for a 750ml of vodka. You can adjust to make less if desired. The keys to achieving a high quality "Mexican Chili Mocha Infused Vodka" are in the quality of coffee beans and cocoa powder you use. You can pick up your favorite beans from your grocery store or even at a Starbucks.

Dark roasted beans have a stronger flavor which in turn gives a stronger infusion. However, use whatever beans you like. One key to infusing coffee beans is to crack open the beans, not necessarily crush them.

On the cocoa powder, strive to get the best you can. Ghirardelli makes a good quality cocoa powder and Scharffen Berger is a good one too. If you are having a hard time finding these, check out Amazon for a wide selection of quality cocoa powders.

Ingredients

½ cup dark roasted coffee beans, lightly cracked

½ cup cocoa powder

2 chili de arbol peppers, crushed

¼ teaspoon paprika

¼ teaspoon cayenne pepper

1 750ml bottle of vodka

Directions

Place the cracked coffee beans, cocoa powder, crushed red chilies, the paprika and cayenne pepper in a clean jar and fill with vodka. Seal the jar and shake really well until contents are thoroughly mixed. Place in a cool place away from direct sunlight for 2 to 4 days. Give the infusion a taste to see how the infusion is coming along. You can allow the infusion to go longer to achieve a stronger flavor. Once the infused vodka has attained the desired flavor, strain the vodka through a coffee filter to remove the ingredients and re-bottle.

DENNIS WALLER

NOTES

CHAPTER NINE
EXOTIC FRUIT INFUSED VODKA

Rambutan Infused Vodka

This recipe is for a 375ml of vodka. You can adjust to make less if desired.

Rambutan is a tasty fruit and it is very popular in many countries throughout Southeast Asia. They are about the size of a golf ball. The mild sweet flavor is a cross between a grape and lychee. Open the fruit by removing part of its skin. Then peel the skin off to reveal the Rambutan. There is a sizable pit in the center and can be removed in the same manner that you would remove the pit from a mango.

Ingredients

2 Rambutan fruits, peeled and pitted

1 375ml bottle of vodka

Directions

Place the Rambutan fruits in a clean jar and fill with vodka. Seal the jar and shake really well until contents are thoroughly mixed. Place in the refrigerator for 5 to 7 days. Once the infusion has attained the desired flavor, strain the vodka through a coffee filter to remove the ingredients and re-bottle.

Dragonfruit Infused Vodka

This recipe is for a 750ml of vodka. You can adjust to make less if desired.

The Dragonfruit is a tasty fruit and it is very popular in many countries throughout Southeast Asia as well as Mexico and Central America. They are about the size of a baseball. The mild sweet flavor is a cross between a kiwi and a pear. Cut the fruit in half straight down the middle. Inside, the flesh will be white or red with tiny black seeds that are edible just like the kiwi. Using a tablespoon, remove the flesh from the skin. Remove any remnants of the skin from the flesh. Cut the flesh into one inch cubes and your Dragonfruit is ready for the infusion.

Ingredients

1 Dragonfruit, prepared as above

1 750ml bottle of vodka

Directions

Place the prepared Dragonfruit in a clean jar and fill with vodka. Seal the jar and shake really well until contents are thoroughly mixed. Place in the refrigerator for 5 to 7 days. Once the infusion has attained the desired flavor, strain the vodka through a coffee filter to remove the ingredients and re-bottle.

Passion Fruit Infused Vodka

This recipe is for a 375ml of vodka. You can adjust to make less if desired.

To prepare the passion fruit, cut in half and remove the pulp. You may leave the seeds in the pulp. The pulp is sweet and tangy and the edible seeds are bitter. You can press the pulp through a sieve to remove the seeds. Either way, passion fruit makes for an interesting infused vodka.

Ingredients

The pulp from 3 Passion fruits

1 375ml bottle of vodka

Directions

Place the passion fruit pulp (with or without the seeds) in a clean jar and fill with vodka. Seal the jar and shake really well until contents are thoroughly mixed. Place in the refrigerator for 5 to 7 days. Once the infusion has attained the desired flavor, strain the vodka through a coffee filter to remove the ingredients and re-bottle.

Lychee Infused Vodka

This recipe is for a 375ml of vodka. You can adjust to make less if desired.

The Lychee has a taste that reminds me of a sweet honeydew melon with a hint of grape. It is now grown in the US and available at finer grocery stores.

The lychee fruit is about 1½ to 2 inches in size, oval to rounded heart shaped and the bumpy skin is red in color. Once you peel the skin off, the crisp juicy flesh of a lychee fruit is white or pinkish, translucent and glossy like the consistency of a grape, but the taste is sweeter.

Lychees have a sub acid sweet taste and have a wonderful freshness to them that is hard to describe. Lychee fruit is high in the antioxidant Vitamin C and the essential mineral Potassium. To prepare the Lychee, peel the fruit and cut out the pit and discard. Use the flesh of the Lychee for the infusion

Ingredients

4 Lychee fruits, peeled and pitted

1 375ml bottle of vodka

Directions

Place the Lychee fruit in a clean jar and fill with vodka. Seal the jar and shake really well until contents are thoroughly mixed. Place in the refrigerator for 5 to 7 days. Once the infusion has attained the desired flavor, strain the vodka through a coffee filter to remove the ingredients and re-bottle.

Horn Melon Infused Vodka

This recipe is for a 375ml of vodka. You can adjust to make less if desired.

The Horn Melon has a taste of cucumber, banana, and lime all combined.

To prepare the horn melon, cut in half and remove the green seedy pulp. You may leave the seeds in the pulp as they have a bland taste. The seeds are edible and will not affect your infusion. The lemon zest and mint leaves help in bringing out the flavor of the horn melon giving you a unique infused vodka

Ingredients

The pulp from 1 Horn Melon

Zest of half of a lemon

4 fresh mint leaves

1 375ml bottle of vodka

Directions

Place the horn melon, zest, and mint leaves in a clean jar and fill with vodka. Seal the jar and shake really well until contents are thoroughly mixed. Place in the refrigerator for 5 to 7 days. Once the infusion has attained the desired flavor, strain the vodka through a coffee filter to remove the ingredients and re-bottle.

Kumquat Infused Vodka

This recipe is for a 375ml of vodka. You can adjust to make less if desired.

The kumquat is similar to the orange except smaller and the peeling of the kumquat is not only edible but has a unique flavor, making for a sweet and tangy taste. In making kumquat infused vodka, we'll use the entire fruit. While not as exotic has it once was, the kumquat can still be a challenge to find.

Ingredients

1 cup Kumquats, washed and quartered

1 375ml bottle of vodka

Directions

Place the quartered Kumquats in a clean jar and fill with vodka. Seal the jar and shake really well until contents are thoroughly mixed. Place in the refrigerator for 3 to 5 days. Once the infusion has attained the desired flavor, strain the vodka through a coffee filter to remove the ingredients and re-bottle.

Pepino Melon Infused Vodka

This recipe is for a 375ml of vodka. You can adjust to make less if desired.

The Pepino melon has a combined taste of cantaloupe and honeydew melon. You would prepare the Pepino melon the same way you would prepare a cantaloupe. Cut in half, remove any seeds, peel off the rind and cube. Interestingly, the Pepino melon isn't related to the melon family. It's related to the tomato and eggplant families.

Ingredients

2 Pepino melons, washed peeled, cleaned and cubed

1 375ml bottle of vodka

Directions

Place the cubed Pepino melon in a clean jar and fill with vodka. Seal the jar and shake really well until contents are thoroughly mixed. Place in the refrigerator for 5 to 7 days. Once the infusion has attained the desired flavor, strain the vodka through a coffee filter to remove the ingredients and re-bottle.

CHAPTER TEN
OTHER TEXAS JACK RECIPE BOOKS

Texas Jack's Famous Caramels Secret Recipe Book

ASIN: B00FIHQ1CQ

This recipe book has a total of 21+ recipes focusing on Texas Jack's Famous Caramels. What makes this recipe book different is it is easy to follow and understand. Including a wide variety of over 14 caramel recipes from Traditional caramels to Pumpkin Spice caramel, Bourbon Chocolate caramel to the crazy delicious Wild Turkey with Honey caramel, these are sure to please everyone. There are also 4 Fudge recipes including the "Andes" Chocolate Mint Fudge and a "Fast and Simple" Fudge with only two ingredients that is so easy to make, you'll be making this one right away.

Along with the caramel and fudge recipes, there is a recipe on how to make the "Fruteria" series of Texas Jack's Famous Pralines. The recipes for these pralines incorporate the use of dried fruits like Mango, Papaya, Cantaloupe, Pineapple or Dates to create a delightful new twist on an old southern favorite. Also included is a recipe for Pumpkin Spice and Apple Spice Pecan Pralines, sure to be a Holiday Favorites this year.

Texas Jack's Famous Pralines Secret Recipe Book

ASIN: B00BLOPWV6

A Praline is a Sweet Southern Treat made up of sugar, cream, vanilla extract, and pecans that can be compared to fudge. This treat is famous throughout the South and over the years, there have been many variations of pralines made. The praline recipes in this book are easy to follow and easier to make using everything from chocolate, coconut, macadamia nuts, almonds, ginger, Amaretto, to Spice Rum.

This is a recipe book containing 12 great different recipes for making Pralines that you can change to make them your own by replacing the flavorings and nuts to whatever suits your fancy. There are also 4 cookie recipes, 4 fudge recipes, and a recipe for making Aunt Bill's Brown Candy and if you have never had Aunt Bill's Brown Candy, well, you aint living, so here is the recipe and get busy living!

Included in this book is the recipe for the all-time favorite, Texas Jack's Calico Cookies. These will leave a smile on your face and a sure bet to please any company that might come calling, so get back to better simpler times and enjoy some Old Fashion Southern Treats!

Texas Jack's Famous Sweet Potato Recipes

ASIN: B00GM11FJQ

This edition focuses on a Southern favorite, the sweet potato. There are over 25 different recipes including recipes for pies, casseroles, mash, hash, cupcakes, even a sweet potato cornbread and biscuits. With easy to follow recipes, this will become a "go to" book for the chef desiring to create a wonderful dessert using sweet potatoes.

Yummy and Sweet Potatoes go together like peas and carrots. This is a vegetable that can be utilized all year long to create some of the most delightfully delicious desserts that you have ever had. Have some fun and cook up a sweet potato dish that will sure to become a family favorite. Enjoy!

Texas Jack's Famous Christmas Pie Recipes

ASIN: B00HCZUUKQ

This edition focuses on 27 different pie recipes offering an excellent variety of choices for the holidays. From the classic Texas Jack's Brown Butter Pecan Pie to a Lemon Coconut Buttermilk Pie, there is something here for everyone. Lovers of chocolate, sweet potatoes, pumpkin, walnuts, key lime, and more will be pleased with these easy to make pies. Yummy Delicious for sure!

Texas Jack's Famous Apple Cider Recipes

ASIN: B00KUYBBYA

Apple cider and the making of apple cider are as much of our American Heritage as baseball and apple pie. Wow, seems these apples play an important part of our history, eh? Interestingly enough, President John Adams on just about every day of his adult life, started it off with a tankard of apple cider. When asked, his reply was, "To do me good." Must have been something to it as he lived to be 91 years old. Now to be clear here, drinking apple cider every day may or may not add to your longevity, but either way, it will certainly make life more enjoyable.

This recipe book contains recipes for making your own Sweet Apple Cider, Hard Apple Cider, and recipes for Apple Cider Smoothies, Hot Apple Cider Drinks, and a variety of Apple Cider Punches. Nothing fancy, just easy recipes that just about anyone can follow. Another excellent aspect to this book is it will keep you out of trouble with grandma. Like she said, "I'll squeeze the cider out of your adam's apple if you don't behave." With this recipe book, no worries just give her a big glass of good old apple cider, or maybe the whole jug just to be safe. Enjoy!

Texas Jack's Famous Smoothie Recipes

ASIN: B00L1BBZWE

The only limit to making smoothies is your imagination. You can make then as sweet or as tart as you want. You can make then extremely healthy or sinfully delightful. You have the ability to make your smoothie to fit the mood at the moment, the power to create whatever your heart desires.

An excellent aspect to smoothies is they are great as a breakfast drink, a dessert, or a mid-day snack. Plus the range of ingredients is boundless. There is nothing too strange that you can't use. Well, maybe. I don't think I would like an Anchovy and Sardine smoothie but that doesn't mean someone wouldn't like one. Either way, there is a recipe for that too.

However, the greatest aspect to the art of smoothies is the Health Benefits they can provide. Smoothies are an excellent source for fiber and nutrients. Drinking a healthy smoothie will provide you with a ton of good stuff for you in a most delicious way. Consuming raw fruits and vegetables helps in keeping you hydrated, providing your body with much needed fuel, and making your digestive track happy.

Well with all of that and without further ado, let's get started making some delightful and delicious smoothies.

NOTES

CHAPTER ELEVEN
A BRIEF HISTORY OF THE ORIGINAL
TEXAS JACK

Now Texas Jack Vermillion was a real live Gunslinger who rode with the Earp's in the "Vendetta Ride" just like in the movie. He was One Bad Hombre for sure and certainly was a friend to Doc Holliday.

John Wilson Vermillion, known as Texas Jack Vermillion (also known as Shoot-your-eye-out-Jack) was born 1842, Russell Co. Virginia. He was the second of 12 children born to William Vermillion and Nancy Owens. When the Civil War erupted in 1861, Texas Jack joined the Confederate cavalry under the command of General J.E.B. Stuart.

After the war Texas Jack married Margaret Horton on September 6, 1865 in Sullivan Co., Tennessee. The newlyweds moved to eastern Missouri where Jack accepted the position as Territorial Marshal for the eastern section of Missouri.

A daughter was born and named Mary and a second child followed. His name is unknown. Within a few weeks of the son's birth and while Jack was away from the home a diphtheria epidemic rambled across eastern Missouri killing Margaret and the children.

It has been written that grief stricken, Jack moved west. He surfaced in Dodge City, Kansas were he drank heavily, gambled frequently thus gaining a reputation as a "devil-may-care" gunslinger. It has also been written that when Dodge City burned for the first time that City Marshal and Deputy U.S. Marshal

Virgil Earp rounded-up 23 men he could trust to prevent lot jumpers. One of those men was Jack Vermillion.

Family history tells a story that Jack turned up in Montana and became involved in a saloon fight. Jack wasn't doing so well until someone stepped in to help. That someone was Doc Holliday. The legend continues that many years later Jack received a trunk shipped to him from Holliday.

As portrayed in the movie **Tombstone**, it has been written that Jack killed a man who accused him of cheating at cards. Unlike the movie, the gunfight was viewed as unfair and Jack became a wanted man. It was on the wanted poster that his name first appeared as "Texas Jack" Vermillion.

Texas Jack rode with Wyatt Earp during his vendetta ride and again was with Wyatt during the Dodge City War. He was considered a crack-shot with a gun by those who knew him.

Vermillion joined up with the Soapy Smith gang in 1888 or 1889, and was involved in the Pocatello, Idaho train depot shoot-out, in which a rival gang was trying to kill Soapy. He disappeared from known gang movements, but was reportedly involved in another gunfight in 1890.

In 1911 Jack passed away quietly in his sleep. It is rumored that his last meal was a praline.

*sourced
<http://captyak.tripod.com/texasjackvermillion/>

Here is another bit of history- "Texas Jack Vermillion did not accompany Virgil Earp as a member of the protective squad which escorted him to Tucson, March 20, 1882. Instead, Vermillion joined the vendetta posse March 21, 1882 in Tombstone, a day after the killing of Frank Stillwell in Tucson, thus Vermillion was not one of the 5 men indicted for Stilwell's killing. He presumably did participate in the killing of Florentino Cruz on March 22, and he had his horse shot out from under him during the fight at Iron Springs (March 24), in which "Curley Bill" Brocius was killed. Vermillion was himself not hit in that fight, but he had to be picked up by Doc Holliday after exposing himself to fire from the cowboys, while trying to retrieve the rifle wedged under his fallen horse."

*sourced   -
<http://en.wikipedia.org/wiki/Texas_Jack_Vermillion>

DENNIS WALLER

ABOUT DENNIS WALLER

Dennis Waller, bestselling author, film maker and speaker, is recognized as an authority on Buddhism, Zen and the Tao Te Ching. His translation of the Tao has been a long standing best seller and is used throughout the academic world. He is only the second person to translate Nagarjuna's Tree of Wisdom into English since WL Campbell's translation in 1919.

He also is known for his series of "Texas Jack's Famous Recipe books, a collection of southern recipes that have been #1 best sellers on Amazon. From pralines, caramels, to making your own hard apple cider, the Texas Jack series has built up a strong and loyal following.

His current project, "In Search of The Kushtaka" released in April 2014 is a book offering different points of view from supporters and critics of the mythical creature, the Kushtaka, of the Tlingit People of Alaska. Covering the Tlingit and comparative mythologies along with thoughts from the science community and firsthand accounts of encounters with the Kushtaka, this book gives an enlightening look into the phenomena known as the Kushtaka.

In addition to the Kushtaka book, he has followed up with two more books on the myths of the Tlingit called, "Raven Tales" and "Otter Tales." Working with the legendary artist of Native American Art, Bob Patterson, Waller will be bringing out an illustrated guide to the world of the myths and legends of the Tlingit in late 2014.

NOTES

NOTES